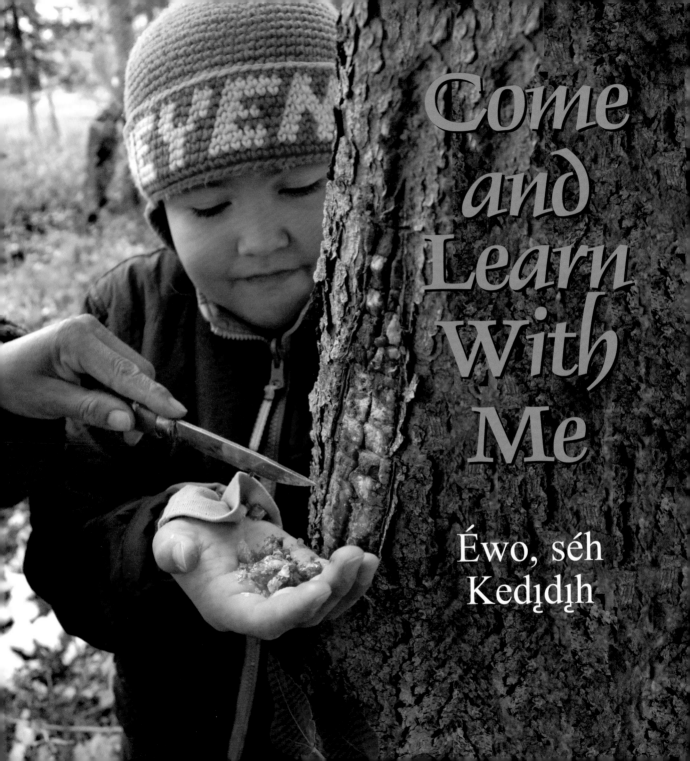

Come and Learn With Me

Éwo, séh Kedįdįh

Fifth House Ltd.
A Fitzhenry & Whiteside Company
195 Allstate Parkway
Markham, Ontario L3R 4T8
1-800-387-9776
www.fitzhenry.ca

CANADIAN NORTH
seriously northern

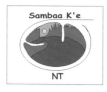

CIBC

Northwest
Territories Education, Culture and Employment

Sambaa K'e

NT

FSC
MIX
Paper from
responsible sources
FSC® C016245
www.fsc.org

First published in the
United States in 2010 by
Fitzhenry & Whiteside
311 Washington Street
Brighton, Massachusetts,
02135

Cover and interior design by John Luckhurst
Photography by Tessa Macintosh
Edited by Meaghan Craven

The type in this book is set in 10-on-15-point Trebuchet Regular and 10-on-13-point Tekton Oblique.

The publisher gratefully acknowledges the support of The Canada Council for the Arts and the Department of Canadian Heritage.

We acknowledge the financial support of the Government of Canada through the Book Publishing Industry Development Program (BPIDP) for our publishing activities.

The authors would like to thank Canadian North, CIBC, the NWT Protected Areas Strategy Secretariat, the Sambaa K'e Dene Band, WWF-Canada and the Government of the Northwest Territories Department of Education Culture and Employment for financial assistance in the completion of this book.

Manufactured by Friesens Corporation in Altona, Canada
October 2009, Job #50212

2020 / 2

Library and Archives Canada Cataloguing in Publication Data

Jumbo, Sheyenne
Come and learn with me = Ewo, seh kedidih /
Sheyenne Jumbo and Mindy Willett.

(The land is our storybook)
ISBN 978-1-897252-57-4

1. Jumbo, Sheyenne—Juvenile literature.
2. Sambaa K'e Dene Band—Juvenile literature.
3. Harvesting—Northwest Territories—Juvenile literature.
4. Autumn—Northwest Territories—Juvenile literature.
5. Trout Lake (N.W.T.)—Biography—Juvenile literature.
I. Willett, Mindy, 1968- II. Title. III.
Title: Ewo, seh kedidih. IV. Series: Land is our storybook

E99.T56J84 2009   j971.9'30049720092   C2009-905447-7

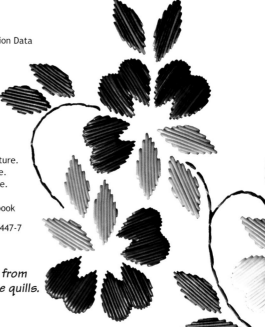

*Flowers made from
dyed porcupine quills.*

Acknowledgements

We would like to thank: Chief Dolphus Jumbo from the Sambaa K'e Dene Band and Grand Chief of the Dehcho Gerald Antoine; Pete Ewins of WWF-Canada, Minister Jackson Lafferty and the Government of the Northwest Territories Department of Education, Culture and Employment, Canadian North Airlines, the NWT Protected Areas Strategy Secretariat, and CIBC for their financial contributions; the community of Trout lake; the students at Charles Tetcho School, Ingrid Kritch for recording the story of Trout Lake, Violet Jumbo and Yvonne Jumbo for doing the translations; Rita Deneron for sharing her knowledge; Judith Drinnan for her ongoing support; Jason Charlwood of Ducks Unlimited Canada; John Stewart, Gladys Norwegian, Tessa Macintosh, and Dianne Lafferty for reviewing the transcript; and George Blondin. Thanks also to the Dene Cultural Institute for their guidance and permission to print the Dene laws.

Sheyenne has many experts and teachers in her life who graciously shared their skills including: her mother, Ruby Jumbo, whose unwavering support has ensured this book's success; her siblings Branden and Shannon; Grandma Emily Jumbo and Grandpa David Jumbo, for sharing all their knowledge about moose and travelling; Victor Jumbo, for amazing us all with his skills making spruce root canoes, snowshoes, and toboggans; Margaret Jumbo, for sharing her drymeat skills, as well as storytelling; Uncle Ralph Sanguez, for teaching drumming; Phoebe Punch, for sharing her incredible skills at making spruce root baskets and her knowledge on plant harvesting for medicines; Norma Jumbo, for teaching Sheyenne about making birchbark baskets; Jessica Jumbo, for taking Sheyenne snaring rabbits; Sheyenne's dad, Terrence Crothers, and the teachers at the school including Maria Jones, Beaver volunteer Sharon Henderson, and Elizabeth von Rhedey. Thanks also to Sheyenne's cousins Corey Jumbo and McKayla Thwaites.

Mindy would like to thank her husband, Damian Panayi, and her two children, Jack and Rae Panayi, for supporting her when she's gone for long periods to work on the books. She really hopes they help her children learn more about the place they call home.

Mindy and Sheyenne are also indebted to Tessa Macintosh for her incredible photographic skills and for making this project so fun to work on; and to Charlene Dobmeier and Meaghan Craven of Fifth House Publishers for listening, being patient and respectful, and ensuring the book reflects the wishes of the community.

For my mom, grandparents, and great-grandparents for teaching me about our culture. Thanks also to the community of Trout Lake. I love living here.

Come and Learn With Me

Éwo, séh Kedįdįh

By **SHEYENNE JUMBO** *and* **MINDY WILLETT**
Photographs by **Tessa Macintosh**

FIFTH
HOUSE

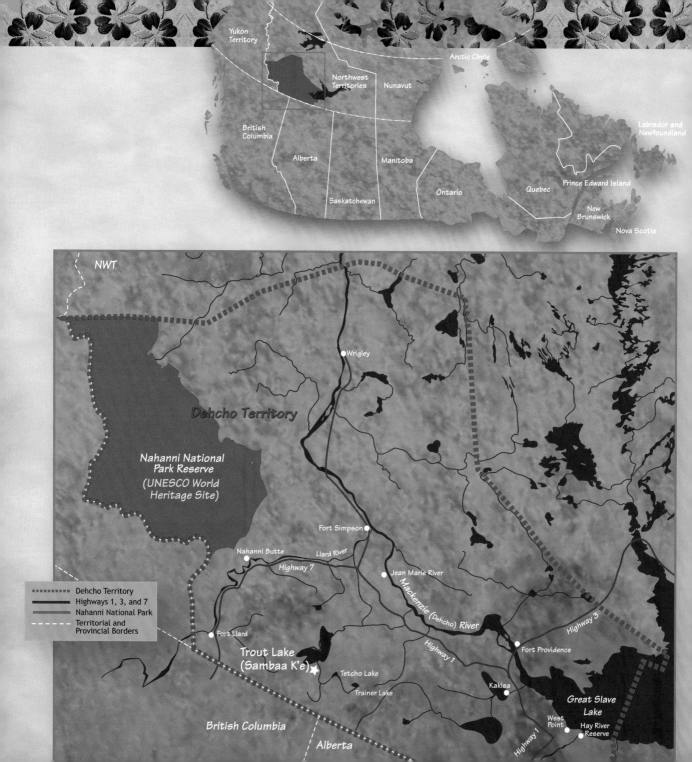

Yukon Territory

Arctic Circle

Northwest Territories

Nunavut

British Columbia

Alberta

Saskatchewan

Manitoba

Ontario

Quebec

Labrador and Newfoundland

Prince Edward Island

New Brunswick

Nova Scotia

NWT

Wrigley

Dehcho Territory

Nahanni National Park Reserve
(UNESCO World Heritage Site)

Fort Simpson

Nahanni Butte

Liard River

Highway 7

Jean Marie River

Mackenzie (Dehcho) River

Fort Liard

Trout Lake
(Sambaa K'e)

Tetcho Lake

Trainer Lake

Highway 1

Highway 3

Fort Providence

Kakisa

Great Slave Lake

West Point

Hay River Reserve

Highway 1

British Columbia

Alberta

Dehcho Territory
Highways 1, 3, and 7
Nahanni National Park
Territorial and Provincial Borders

Ndegha dágondíh,

Sheyenne Jumbo súye. I am the daughter of Ruby Jumbo, and my grandparents are David and Emily Jumbo.

I'm nine years old and in Grade 5. I have a six-year-old brother named Branden and my baby sister Shannon just turned one.

We live in Sambaa K'e, or Trout Lake, which is a small community in the Decho Region of the Northwest Territories. There are about seventy-five or eighty people in our town. Others come to visit here as our Elders have lots of skills and the fishing is really good.

It's fall time now, the season of moose, and I've got lots to learn. The school is closed for the next two weeks for our Cultural Days. Come and learn with me as I take you on a tour of our town and introduce you to some of the experts in my community.

Mahsi cho,

Sheyenne

Sheyenne Jumbo

Meet My Family

In Sambaa K'e, I have lots of aunties and uncles and cousins. My grandparents live near my house. I just have to go out my door and walk through a little path in the bush to their house. It only takes me a couple of minutes. I like to spend lots of time with them.

This is Sheyenne's family. She's shown here with her mother, Ruby, brother, Branden, and little sister, Shannon.

Sheyenne's mom and her grandma, Emily, have taught her to make bannock. Her little sister, Shannon, loves to eat it, especially when it's fresh out of the oven with homemade blueberry jam.

The rest of my family isn't far either, as my town isn't that big. Sometimes I go visit my aunties, uncles, and cousins. My dad, Terry, lives in town, too, but not with us. I like to play sports and music with him at the community gym. It's open in the evenings, so people can hang out there.

Left: Sheyenne's cousin, Jessica, has shown her how to snare a rabbit.

Branden is playing with a bow and arrow made for him by his uncle, Ralph.

3

My town is named after the lake we live on. There are lots of trout in our lake, and they can get really, really big. Many tourists come here to fish. We have a lodge on our lake, too.

I can't remember the first time I caught a fish, but the last time I caught one I almost lost it because it was too strong. It was big. My grandpa David helped me reel it in and scoop it with the net.

We often make dried fish with all the fish we catch so we can store the fish for a long time. It's yummy with salt and pepper.

Our Flag

Our flag has a picture of a fish head for a few reasons. One is that the name of our town is Trout Lake—fish are important to us. But if you look closely, you'll also see that the trout head is made up of a river and islands. This is because our town is located at the mouth of the Among-the-Islands River, or Ndu Tah. Our town is on the part of the lake where the river flows out.

My house is the one with the arrow pointing to it!

Sambaa K'e

NT

The wind can come up quickly over the lake, so we have to be careful when we're out there. My grandpa, who has lived here all his life, has taught me how to watch the wind so I will know when it's safe to travel by boat. He showed me how to read the waves to know if they will be bigger out in the middle of the lake than they appear on shore.

Sheyenne's grandpa, David, is taking her out on the lake. She has learned that if you don't respect the lake and give it thanks, the weather will turn. To show respect, she offers something to the lake, whatever she happens to have on her. Even a piece of thread tied to a trailing willow branch will help the lake waters stay calm.

Our town has a general store, band office, school, community complex, municipal garage, and a small hotel for people who come to visit. Our groceries, mail, and library books come in by plane. In the winter, we drive out of town on the winter ice road. In the summer we leave our truck in Fort Simpson. If we want to leave Trout Lake, we charter a plane and pick up our truck when we get there.

Trout Lake has a big community garden. The potatoes and onions grown here are sold in the general store, which is also the post office.

Ruby Jumbo, Sheyenne's mom, went to residential school in Yellowknife and then Northern Alberta Institute of Technology in Edmonton. As band manager, she is very busy coordinating all the programs for the community.

Sheyenne's Uncle Ralph has organized a wiener roast in the gazebo outside Sheyenne's house. After a bite to eat, Ralph takes out his drum and teaches everyone a traditional song.

My best friend is Katrina. We love to run around town, go camping, play at the beach, roast marshmallows, make forts, and build sandcastles. In the winter we like to drive around on our snowmobiles.

Sheyenne and Katrina turned the living room into a store.

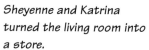

When I'm not playing with my friends, I like to write in my journal. Robert Munsch once came to our school. His book *Smelly Socks* inspired me to write. It reminded me of my town because we can't buy socks here. I wrote a similar story called *Clean Socks*.

In a little town called Big Fish there was a girl. Her name was Ashley. Ashley woke up one morning and said to her mother, "I need nice new clean socks. Can we go to town to buy socks? Please, oh please?" Ashley's mom, Selena, said, "Now how can we go to town? We don't have the money to afford a plane." "Okay, I will just have to wait until someone goes to town then I can go on the plane with them," Ashley said to her mom.

On Friday, a plane was coming in from Hay River and there were seats for two people to go on the plane back. Ashley asked her mom if they could both go and her mom said okay. When they got there, Ashley said, "Can we go to the Northern store to buy socks please?" "We will go there after," Selena said. They went to the food store, the drug store, Joey's, Fields, Home Hardware, and True Value. By the time it was time to go to the Northern it was closed.

On Saturday morning they went to the Northern and it was open. Selena said to Ashley, "Now, we can't stay too long because we are leaving on the plane at 12:00 pm and we only have half an hour." "Sure, okay," Ashley said.

Ashley went to the sock aisle and while she was choosing the socks she wanted, she said, "Socks, socks, wonderful socks, dotted socks, spotted socks, striped socks. I love socks!" Finally she was done. Then Selena looked at the time and said, "We have six minutes to get to the airport." So they paid for the socks and took off to the airport. They were on their way back to Big Fish. Ashley fell asleep and dreamed of her wonderful new clean socks.

I go to the Charles Tetcho School. Our teacher's name is Mrs. Jones. She says I'm a good reader. One time I won a contest because I read the most out of anyone in the NWT. I read twenty minutes every day for seventeen weeks without missing one day!

Although I like to read, my favourite subject is math because when you do problem solving you get to draw pictures, and I really like learning the times table.

Mrs. Jones is the classroom teacher who teaches most of the subjects for student from K-9. They are all in one classroom together. Yvonne Jumbo teaches culture and language.

At Charles Tetcho School, each child works at his/her own pace. Sheyenne is the only student in Grade 5. The school has a few computers with Internet access.

Our traditional language is Dene Yatie. My mom speaks our language with my grandparents and with other people in town. I can understand what she's saying, and when my grandma asks me for things in our language, I know what she wants. But I am shy to speak it myself. We are learning the language in school, too, and each morning we sing "O Canada" in Dene Yatie.

Our Words
"O Canada" in Dene Yatie

O Canada!
  Our home and native land!

True patriot love
  in all thy sons command.

With glowing hearts,
  we see thee rise,

The True North
  strong and free!

From far and wide,
  O Canada,

We stand on guard
  for thee.

God keep our land
  glorious and free.

O Canada
  We stand on guard for thee.

O Canada
  We stand on guard for thee.

O Canada!
  Ndahe-kų́ę́ gots'ęh
  ndahe-ndee

Ehtth'ı tá'h ndeghǫndıethıto

Ndahe-dzee t'áh ndahegha
  gonezų

Ndahe-ndehé nechá gots'ęh
  ndátse

Nidhą́ą́ ahthít'e,
  O Canada,

Ndegha
  Ndadehthiya.

Noohtsıne ndahe-ndéhé
  k'éondıh

O Canada,
  Ndegha ndadehthiya.

O Canada,
  Ndegha ndadehthiya.

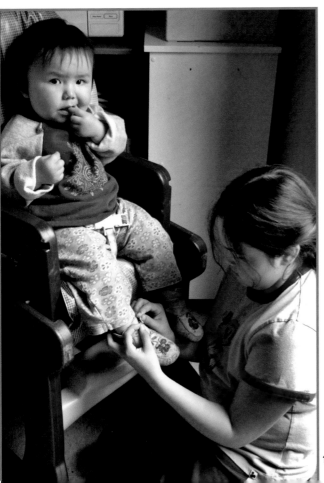

Sheyenne teaches her baby sister some Dene words. Shannon can already say "ná," which means "here, take it" and "dé," which means "give it to me."

This year, Mrs. Jones encouraged me to enter a writing contest called "Canada Writes to Read." I was the grand prize winner for the NWT with my story of how Trout Lake was formed by the giant, *Godǫhlecho*. My story was published with all the other provincial and territorial winners in a book called, *The Write to Read Collection*.

My mom told me the story about how Trout Lake was formed. It was told to her by her grandma, Madeline Tetcho, who is my great-grandma. My story is a short version of the story, and it is positively true. We have lots of stories that explain how the land was formed around here.

A sun dog (dahadeh k'ale) on Trout Lake.

Our Stories
The Giant Who Formed Trout Lake
by *Sheyenne Britney Jumbo*

A long time ago, before our time, Trout Lake was formed by *Godǫhlecho*, the giant. He was a nice giant. He had a brother named *Yambahdéyaa*. The two brothers both went separate ways. *Yambahdéyaa* went south and *Godǫhlecho* came north. That's when *Godǫhlecho* decided to have a drink. He scooped up water to drink with a bowl and that formed Trainer Lake. What he scooped up he put aside, and that is a hill. After the drink, he took a nap in the muskeg. A short while after he lay down to rest, a muskrat wanted to get by the sleeping giant, so the muskrat bit the giant's ankle vein. The blood is still there. The giant felt pain so he stretched out his leg. That's why at the south of the lake there is a long bay. When he stood up, he left his shape in the muskeg, which became *Sambaa K'e*.

Check out the shape of Trout Lake on the map at the beginning of the book.

Godęhlecho's brother, Yambahdéyaa, is known as the "one who circled the earth." He made the world safe and gave all Dene people the laws that they live by. He left signs on the land where he travelled. In Nahanni National Park there is a place called Gah Teni, or Rabbit Kettle. Yambahdéyaa's house is a large white rock and his dishes are rocks with saucer-shaped indentations. People say they can still hear him walking on the rocks at night.

Although we are learning a bit about our language in school, I mostly hear our language when I spend time with my Elders, like during Cultural Days. It is a very busy time of year. In the fall we hunt moose and then make drymeat. My pieces of drymeat are so small compared to my grandmother's, but she is happy when I try.

Sometimes the hunters go out in a plane to get the moose. Every family needs a few moose to feed them during the winter.

Even very young children are encouraged to be around and help out. Sheyenne's little cousin McKayla's little pieces of drymeat are only 10 cm long but are still hung up on the pole to dry.

www.yukon-wings.com

CF-FHZ

To make drymeat, thin, large slices of meat are cut up and hung over a fire. The smoke keeps the bugs away and makes the meat taste good. This is one way to preserve the meat. It is stored for use over the winter.

My grandmother uses the hides to make many things like moccasins, jackets, and dolls. It's a lot of work, so we all have to help out.

First the hair needs to be taken off. When all the hair is removed, my grandmother places the hide on a wooden stretcher, so she can scrape off the sinew and tendons and bits of hair that might still be on the hide. The scraping makes the hide an even thickness. After scraping she tans the hide.

Left: Preparing a moose hide for sewing material is a lot of hard work.

Emily's homemade moose-hide doll has flowers on the jacket made from moose hair that she has dyed and tufted. To make the tufts, she groups hairs together and passes a thread through the backing around the bundle, pulling it tight. This makes the bundle stand up into a tuft, which is then knotted. Emily then trims the tuft into a rounded shape.

When we're harvesting moose in the bush camp, there is lots of time to do other things, like make stuff from birchbark. When I was little, my cousin, Norma, taught me how to make a basket. You need flattened birchbark, spruce roots, porcupine quills, and something to poke holes in the bark. I'm still learning, but I don't like using the quills. They hurt my fingers.

Famous Baskets

Birchbark and spruce-root containers have been used for centuries by the people of the Dehcho for carrying water and berries and even for cooking. Spruce root was used to hold the pieces together, and baskets were made waterproof with spruce gum. Today these incredible baskets are decorated with dyed porcupine quills and are mostly made to sell.

Norma Jumbo makes her living selling baskets. Here she is soaking the quills in her mouth and pulling them through the bark. She'll put another piece of bark over the quills when she's done so you can't see the back of the quills.

To finish off the basket Norma pokes holes in the bark with an awl and uses spruce root and sinew to hold it together.

S pruce roots can be used to make an entire basket. First, you have to find a medium-sized tree with straight, long limbs. Dig down into the mossy area at the base of the tree. Dig until you find a straight, long root that is easy to split. Cut this root from the tree, and then put the moss back so you won't hurt the tree. Keep the root coiled and in a plastic bag to keep it moist. If it gets dry before you use it, you'll need to soak it in water.

Above: Roots are gathered from white spruce trees in June through September as the bark strips off the root easier during the summer. They are then split in half.

Spruce-root baskets were once common but the craft died out when European traders brought copper kettles and pots to the North. A Dene woman, Suzan Marie, saw a picture of one in a museum. She worked with other women to revitalize the tradition. Here, Sheyenne is making a basket with Phoebe Punch.

An awl is used to make a hole for the roots to go through. The awl comes from the ankle bone of a moose.

1 Dahtheht'oh
　　Yarrow
Boil it and strain it. The tea is good for sore throats and chest colds.

2 Ichuh
　　Rose hips
Good for eating when ripe in fall. Spit out the seeds. Boil and strain to remove seeds and make jam. Good for colds.

3 Idzea tl'uhé
　　Strawberry runner
Helps when you have heart burn.

4 Mbehddhii jie
　　Juniper or owl berries
When you are out on the land, eat these berries and you won't feel thirsty. Keep them in your freezer and eat one a day for good health.

5 Ts'u dhené
　　Spruce tree fungus
Let it burn in your house to help you get rid of a headache.

When we're out in the bush during the fall, knowledgeable people from our community gather plant medicines. I don't know very much about these things yet, but Phoebe Punch sure does. Phoebe has taught me about certain plants, and I've learned a lot from her. Now I can share what I know with you.

Only trained people should use plant medicines. Phoebe told Sheyenne that you have to make sure you know what you're doing because plants can be very powerful and can cause you harm if you use them incorrectly.

❻ Ts'u dzeh
   Spruce gum

Remove gum from tree, put on cuts to help heal and reduce infection. Used as glue to waterproof baskets and canoes.

❼ Dehgoné'
   Dry swan willow

Boil the leaves and bark and drink the juice or apply it to sores. Good for chest cold and congestion.

❽ Gots'itagoo tú
   Labrador tea leaves

Boil it and strain it. The tea is good for sore throats, headaches, and stomach aches.

❾ Ndue t'ue
   Tamarac bark

Peel the bark off then boil it and keep the liquid in a jar in the fridge for when you need it. This is good for a sore throat.

The plants in this picture are laid out on a locally made, bent-willow stick table.

All that fall work—picking berries, snaring rabbits, gathering plants, making baskets, and preparing the moose—means we can have yummy jam and meat throughout the winter. It's not really fall work; it's fall fun!

Sheyenne walks down the road from her house to go back to school after Cultural Days.

Sheyenne picks cranberries (netl'é) with Katrina right outside her house.

When Cultural Days are over, we go back to school and learn different things. I know I'm lucky to have so many teachers to learn from.

Maybe someday I'll be a teacher, too, and you can come and learn with me.

All the Details!

cho – big.

dahadeh k'ale (sun dog) – sun dogs are caused by ice crystals in cirrus clouds or during cold weather. They can appear as a halo around the sun or as two light patches on either side of the sun making it look like there are three suns.

Dé – Give it to me.

deh – river.

Dehcho – Mackenzie River (Big River).

Dene Yatie – part of a language family known as Na-Dene or Athapaskan. Languages related to Dene Yatie are spoken from the northern part of the NWT (Gwich'in) to the south of Arizona. All these languages are from one people but time and distance has shaped the language. Dene Yatie used to be known as South Slavey.

gah – rabbit.

goҩ – moose.

k'itene – birchbark basket.

Ná – Here, take it.

netl'é – cranberries.

Ndegha dágondíh – How are you doing?

Ohndahe – Elder.

Sheyenne Jumbo súye – My name is Sheyenne Jumbo.

xa tene – spruce-root basket.

hat'ąą – autumn.

Yambahdéyaa – He is known by different names in each Dene tribe. The stories told of how he made the land safe and gave the Dene their laws tie the Dene people to the land and to each other. *Yambahdéyaa* is also known as *Yamoozha* (Tłįchǫ), *Yamoria* (Sahtuot'ine Yati), *Atachuukaii* (Gwich'in), and *Yabatheya* (Dene Suline).

The Dene Laws

The following laws belong to all Dene. They are reprinted here with permission from *Medicine Power* by George Blondin, published by the Dene Cultural Institute.

1. You must share with others.
   Sharing is like a tree. There are many branches attached to the central tree or sharing law.
   - Share all the big game you kill.
   - If you catch more fish than you need, share with others.
   - Help elders get firewood and do other heavy work.
   - Help the sick and other people in need to do their work and to get food.
   - Share the sorrow with relatives when someone dies, so families do not mourn alone.
   - Help widows and their children with everything they need.
   - Orphans should be looked after by their parents' next of kin.
   - The leader of each tribe should help travellers in need far from their homeland.

2. Do not run around when elders are eating.

3. Love each other as much as possible.

4. Do not harm people with your actions.

5. Be polite. Do not use words which will hurt people.

6. When children start to talk, parents are to teach them to be good citizens, to love one another, and to use medicine power only to help people in need.

7. Elders should gather each day to teach the laws. Elders must teach children to be citizens and to act like human beings. Elders must tell stories about the past each day because stories shape behaviour and attitude. Through stories about mistakes made in the past and present, elders can prevent people from making mistakes in the future.

(For more information on the Dene Laws go to www.deneculture.org)

Paper Berry Basket

1. Using stiff paper, photocopy the pattern at the size you want the basket to be.

2. Colour and design. For ideas, look at Sheyenne's basket on page 23.

3. Cut out along the dark lines.

4. Fold #2 over #1 so the sewing pattern lines up, and then staple or tape with clear tape. Repeat with #3 over #4.

5. Fold the #6 over the #5s so that the sewing patterns line up, and then staple. Repeat with #8 over the #7s.

6. You should now have a rectangular bottom and a cone-shaped basket.

7. Cut out a round lid to fit the hole at the top of the cone-shaped basket.

8. Punch a hole through the lid and basket. Use string to connect the lid to the basket (or moosehide, if you have it).

9. Fill with your favourite in-season berry!

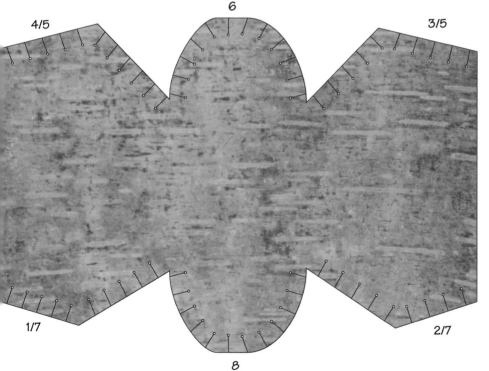

6

4/5

3/5

1/7

2/7

8

About the Authors and Photographer

Sheyenne Jumbo is a nine-year-old storyteller from Sambaa K'e, Northwest Territories. She loves to go sliding, skating, Ski-doing, and camping with her friends and family. She also likes playing guitar, reading, writing in her journal, and telling stories. Sheyenne won the *Canada Writes to Read* contest with her story of how her town, Sambaa K'e, was made by the giant.

Mindy Willett is an educator from Yellowknife. She is currently working on the book series, *The Land is Our Storybook. Come and Learn with Me* is the fourth in the series. Look for the others called, *We Feel Good Out Here, The Delta is My Home,* and *Living Stories.* When not writing she can be found paddling or skiing on Great Slave Lake with her young family.

Tessa Macintosh first came north to Cape Dorset in 1974. A few years later, she headed to Yellowknife to work as a photographer for the *Native Press* and then the NT government. She is now a freelance photographer living in Yellowknife. Her favourite experiences are with people out on the land.